105 POEMS WRITTEN IN 15 MINUTES
AT EDINBURGH YOUTH GAITHERIN
EASTER 2010

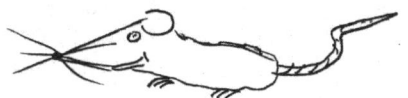

"Mouse Poems

Inspiration on the fly
Published by PoemCatcher Creations
Salisbury Centre
2 Salisbury Road
Edinburgh, EH165AB

Copyright
All the poems in this book were donated with love and permission to be published. It would be thievery to steal the copyright from the authors. It remains their own and I appreciate the privilege of being allowed to publish them. Their creativity is beautiful and inspiring. Use of this material is welcome, providing it inspires, engages and enthrals audiences. It is a lovely courtesy to reference the poet and the book when you use it..

Each and every poem in the book is brilliant,. If you disagree, send £10 with your letter of complaint to a child in Haiti

Cover Design by Trevor at Fresh Digital
ISBN 978-0-9567645-3-9

This book is as quick as a mouse.
It was written in 15 minutes by 105 aspiring musicians
and proves their poetical talents
It is the 11th PoemCatcher book.

Visit www.poemcatcher.com for other titles.
QUAKE – Built from nothing
BALLS from the queue (Wimbledon tennis)
FUNGUS Poems
SALTY poems from the Sea
FANTASTIC FIREWORKS
HAUNTED HALLOWEEN

About PoemCatcher Creations

The pavement PoemCatcher wanders the streets of festivals and events begging for fresh poems to be written "on the fly". Nearly every poem that is donated gets published, creating books with poetic snapshots that capture the public experience and delight the reader.

He has done this since sitting down on a pavement in march 2010 to beg for poems for the people of Haiti.

By spontaneously asking passing public to "DONATE A POEM" he inspires brilliance, encourages "raw creativity" and fundraises for charity.

www.poemcatcher.com
inspiration@poemcatcher.com

Everyone has a mouse story.
Big or small. Friend or foe.

Thank you poets for your creative brilliance
Thank you musicians for your melodies of life.
Thank you mouses for whatever it is you do.

Amazing Poets

Aoife Baskill
Orla Dickson
Meghan McAra
Louise Harris
Mia Scott
Jamie Steele
Roisin Kennelly
Sarah Ramsey
Freya Ruuskanen
Peter Johnston
Ishbel Morton
Caitlin Warrington
Evie Boyd
Florence Reeves
Magnus Turpie
Euan Brownlie
Fergus McMahon
Archie Nicholson
Graeme Platman
Maxim Bird
Alex Rycroft
Rosaly Boyd
Neil MacPherson
Kirsten Forsyth
Iona Steadman
Erin Johnston
Hannah Wyness
Maggie Wilson
Cameron Newell
Keir Logan
Phoebe Hyde
Rosslyn Cole
Natasha Jenkins
Katharine Ruff
Imogen Reeves
Felix Reynish
Ellen Francis
Seona Noble

Finlay Donald Cameron Graham
Hansine Marshall
Eva Moles-Howieson
Malcolm Spence
Amy Baskill
Finn Kennedy
Charlie West
Lucie Hall
Janie Bell
Phoebe O'Carroll-Moran
Orla Steadman
Louis Barbour-McDowell
Kirsten Simpson
Ellen Morton
Lloyd Burden-Garabedian
Oonagh Thin
Micha Cooper
Amina Davidson
Sean Steadman
Florence Jackson
Luke Simpson
Angus Pinsky
Eva Brownlie
Leonore Bergeret
Alastair Salmean
Lucy Girven
Reuben Foran-Gillespie
Tom Campbell
Lachlan Riddell
Angus Brownlie
Keir Hughes
Joe Hathway
Donald Marshall
Ewan Stewart
Lucas Thomson
Naina Woodhouse
Mario Falsone

Thomas Kettle
Luca MacDonald
Roisin Ramsay
Laura Anne MacLeod
Imogen Bose-Ward
Finlay Harry NobleChamings
Zoe MacIntyre
Sam Grassie
Charlotte Gunn
Eilidh Allen
Katie Allen
Catriona Hawksworth
Rhiannon McAra
Elspeth Simpson
Rowan Simpson
Rachel Gray
Christina Bell
Ada Francis
Clare Sterritt
Rhona Stevens
Orla Stevens
Eilidh Hunter
Kirsty Glasgow
Isabella Webster
John Ferrie
Jack McRobbie
Sinead Thin
Ava Molleson
Esther Molleson
Flora McMahon
Olivia Stewart
Lily Crosbie
Milly Hathway
Emma Mason
Finn Croy
Rosie MacLeod

The Mouse

It has two ears and
4 small legs with pointy toes
Its a mouse I say!

By Flora McMahon
aged 11

TRAP

Ewan Stewart 13

The room seemed to be empty,
No-one in sight at all,
It wass all silent as i scurried out my hole,
I jump onto the table,
I jump towards my lunch,
munch, munch, munch, munch, munch, munch, crunch,
Then with a twitch of my ears I hear someone coming,
I jump down from the table,
My heart pounding,
Searching for a hole,
For me to crawl,
My claws skitter though the hole,
Just in the nick of time,
Snap goes the trap

A little wee mouse

A little wee mouse,
Escaped from the house,
He ran up the street,
Away from the feet,
Ran into a cat,
Then hid under a hat,
But the cat tipped the hat,
And that was the end of that

Róisín, 9

MOUSE

Grey or black or maybe brown,
make some people smile,
Some people frown,
they run really fast,
all over your house,
did you know it was there?
aah! there's the mouse!

Eva Moles-Hamieson
12 yrs old

Don't really know what to say about mice even if I think mice

BANG

Norma Whyte
by: ? age: 13

There's a moose in the hall
And he's fat and he's tall,
He's got antlers as big as my arm
He just gallops around,
leaving 'treats' on the ground,
Oh! I do hope this moose is no harm.

He could scare all the children
Like gertrude and Mildred.
I think we better leave it at that,
He could nibble a cable
or pop on the table.
I really wish we had a cat
A wee moose =:)
(Title)

Finlay Graham
12

Mouse

I know a mouse that lives
In a house. He nibbles at the cheese
And never says please. He is very
Rude and is always in a hood.
The people don't know, so they scream
and say "doh." "The little scamp,"
said the tramp "is nearly as smelly as
me!

        Louis Barbour McDonell
        11 years old

MICE

Mice are nice,
but they don't like rice
they eat cheese,
so give them it please.

When you see a mouse
in your house do not
fear the mouse exterminaters
are always near.

by Janie Bell
12

mouse

~~Oh the starving mouse is rolling about the house~~

oh thee starving mouse is
rolling about the house like a
mad whisky grouse oh and
SWap!! ~~the mouse goes~~
The mouse goes.

by Tom Campbell-
paine

age 12

A cute wee mouse,
running around the hoose.
And as I thought,
About when he'll get caught,
I closed the door.
Then I spewed all over the floor

Angus pinsky 9 years old

The Mouse

The Mouse

There once was a mouse in the staff room,
Which the poem catcher tried to hit with a broom
It came down with a crack
and broke its wee back
Now we can eat in the staff room.

Christopher Ferrie
16

Mouse

There once was a Mouse

Who lived in a House.

Who ate Some Cheese

But Never Said please.

Aoife Dashill   13

Mouse in my house

The mouse in my house
Isn't very ~~milk~~ good
'cos he goes and eats all my food
Chocolate bakes, almond paste
He isn't fussy and his name is Luosy.

Aaah! I scream
~~~~ as he chews a beam
How I hope to never see him again.

name: Amy BASKILL

age: 11

Mouse

I have a mouse
It lives in my house
and ~~that's~~ pretty much it ....

John Ferri 15

Ada's cheesy chobs

There once was a mouse called Cheese, who lived underneath my big purple house.
It liked my friend Ada, 'cause she did him a favour, and gave him some cheese from her blouse.

Lily Crosbie 14

Twinkle Twinkle little mouse
Paul McCartney was a souse
~~Up above the world so high,~~
Up above people stand so high,
Like the cheese in the sky,
Twinkle twinkle little mouse,
Please stop living in my house

Imogen Bose-Ward
15

My feelings — Sam Grassie Age 5

I like mice
they are nice

MOUSE = NAH

Mouse, mouse get out of my house
You're not welcome as you are minging and look like a louse.
Why do you eat our food, its ours.
Why do you squeak so much its sends tingles down the spine — I can't ryhme.

Ada, 14,

MOUSE 'squeak'

People run, screaming,
for the safety of a chair or table
Where they can stand, squawking,
until the danger has passed.
Others grab knives, rolling pins, or
fly swatters,
To defend themselves against it
In amongst the pandemonium
the cause of the panic sits
on it's haunches, cleaning it's whiskers,
Nibbling a crumb that it dared to retrieve,
A mouse.

Katharine 13

MOUSE

There once was a mouse,
Who lived in a house,
He ate lots of cheese,
And never said please,
But then one night he got a fright,
And that was the end of the mouse.

IONA STEADMAN Age: 13

The Mouse

with eyes so small
and a nose so pink
this mouse is too fast ~~xxx~~
and it's gone... in a blink

it always has to ~~scurry~~ scurry,
SLOW DOWN!! what's the hurry,
theres plenty of cheese
for us all to share

maggie
wilson   13

TITLE: Mouse, at Dusk

A mouse, at dusk,
~~clears~~ ~~considerately~~
~~on the floor its~~
~~tea,~~ listens quietly
as she tunes her
fiddle, ~~knowing soon~~
~~the kitchen will be~~
~~his~~ considering his
nightly promenade.
Will he scurry to a ~~strathspey?~~ Strathspey?
Run to a reel?
Jump to a jig?
~~Or~~ Or nibble quietly to the
soothing serenade of her slow air.

NAME: CATHY R.

TITLE: Mouse, at Dusk

A mouse, at dusk,
~~hears considerately~~
~~on the feet its~~
~~tea,~~ listens quietly
as she tunes her
fiddle, ~~tapping soon~~
~~the fiddle will be~~
~~his~~ considering his
nightly promenade.
Will he scurry to a ~~strathspey?~~ Strathspey?
Run to a reel?
Jump to a jig?
~~or~~ Or nibble quietly to the
soothing serenade of her slow air.

NAME: CATHY R.

Mouse in the House

My mum screemes when
there's a mouse in the house.
My sister jumps on the bed
and hopes that the mouse is dead.
But even though you might
not beleive, the mouse always
gos for me.   will

By Esther Molleson
Age 9 yrs

Mouse Poem

Little black, beady eyes,
Watching the skies.
He waits for everybody to leave,
Then he can go and rade
the kitchen.
All the cakes, all the
pies and all the fruit,
way up high.
He wishes
that they
could feel
how he did,
then they could
be his friends.

Ava Mollesson 12

The Mouse

The Mouse is a creepy little thing,
he Moves about in a ring-a-ding-
ding, He's a sneeky little fellow, who is
verry Mellow, He'l go around looking
for things, and the thing he wants is
yellow! Yellow   Yellow

Yellow

SQUEEK!

BY Flossy AGE 9

Finn 10 years old

Mouse

There once was a mouse,
In my house.
It was very, very small,
And wasn't ~~tall~~ at all.
It was very dumb,
~~And didn't~~ like my thumb.
It was a boy,
But not a ~~boy~~ boy.
It didn't like biscuits,
But it did like coke.

The big brown Mouse!

The big brown Mouse
Scitters and scatters
right there in his house

He eats lots of cheese
He likes it a lot
but don't look in the fridge
for thats were he eats out of the
Pot!

By Flora McMahon
Aged: 11

MICE

I hate mice, because they're not nice.
I want to feed them peas but I think
they would prefer cheese.
They can do as they please

Katie Allen 15

Letters of a mouse

M is for the mischif in the kitchen

O is for over and over again it eats

U is for the unusual squeeck it makes

S is for the speed it can run into its hole

E is for how much it eats during the day

By Reubin
aged ten

Mouse why are you in my house

Out don't make me shout

Under the door

So very sly ~~Sly out~~

Eating all my tasty pie
good bye mouse stay out my house

Orla age: 11

The Mouse

The mouse played tennis,
it went to Venice,
Its thoughts were
ever so clear,
Its coat was so white,
and ever so light,
but the rodent never
cryed a tear.

Thomas Kettle.
13

~~Why mice aren't good enough~~

If mice played fiddles
And danced a fling
If mice ~~sang sweetly those~~ played pipes
And sweetly died ~~sing~~
Then maybe I would like them
Maybe they'd be nice.
But as it is, I don't like mice.

Amy 18

Not a lot

What to write about a mouse?
He's small and quiet nothing much
Blank pages empty fridge
A single mouse a quiet mouse.

But havoc is caused wherever he is
Upset cats, a disapearing cheese
You never see him not at all
One at a time, there he is.

Not much to say about the mouse
All alone in the empty house.

by,
Eilidh Hunter 14

Amy is a moose

Amy has a moose
it's in her lovely wee hoose
she tried to set it loose
but it stayed.

I've seen the tiny wee moose
scampering around her beautiful hoose
it doesn't want to be set loose
so it stayed.

Amy did not love the moose
she wanted it to leave her hoose
it wouldn't let her set it loose
so it didnae leave.

Amy loved that little moose.

by Kerry Hunter
aged 17
poetic genius

The Mouse

Their was a mouse in the house,
he scurries around the house day & night,
then gives them a fright.
They chase him aound till he gets to a hole,
but the people puts traps outside the hole,
and then he gets STRIKED!

SEAN   Age: 9
STEADMAN

Ginger Mouse

I once knew a ginger haired mouse
He lived in a hole in my house
He had ginger hair,
but then it turned fair
and now hes a strawberry blonde mouse

Fergus McMahon

A Mouse in your house

Is there a mouse in your house?
does that mouse have a louse?
when you buckle your knees,
because it eats all your cheese,
just don't be a big girl's blouse!

Keir Logan   11 years old

THE WEE GUY

There was a wee guy,
Who was kinda shy,
He lived in a hole
but Oh he had soul,
He had lots of courage
when he had a roumage.
through anything that pleased
which always was cheese,

Mario Falsone 13

mousey

Once there was a mouse,
who loved cheese.
but he was very very sad,
because he was lactose-Intolerant
and he couldn't eat cheese
but then one day he ate the cheese
and he exploded

by Rhiannon

Oh Mouse

Oh mouse,
Why do you scamper around
in my house?
I'm afraid I don't have
some cheese,
All I've got is my head,
arms, and knees,
So now I am asking you
please.

Oh mouse,
Why <u>do</u> you scamper around
in my house?

Joe Hathway   - aged 11

MOUSE IN BOOTS

There once was a mouse in a house,
Who had no friends and no spouse.
He wore shiny, black suits
And shiny, black boots
Which sometimes attrackted a louse.

by Phoebe Hyde
age 11

Mice and children.

Mice are like little children.
They're cute, but annoying as well.
Like little children, they snaffle your sweets,
And eat them without feeling guilty.
But children aren't scary, unlike mice,
And they don't run away when you tell them off.
Mice don't scream, kids don't scurry.
What's worse? We'll never know.

By Emma Mason,
       age 12.

mouse trouble

The little old mouse
That lives in our house
Eats all the cheese
never says please

He loves to tease the cat
If he didn't he would get fat
He hides under my bed
Then jumps out on my head

He was under my hat
when up jumps the cat
and that was the end of that

By
Florence C
Jackson
10

Kirsten Forsyth

There was a mouse called Tommy
who had a rumbly tummy!
He'd had a big brunch
but he wanted his lunch
so he had some cheese which was
yummy!

That Muse

Theres a wee muse how Lives in my house. How cralles around Stelling all my Juse. Squiking and ecking all over my food.
Drops of brown all over my ~~bees~~ home.

WHAT WILL I DO WITH THAT LITTLE MUSE!!!
?

EK

Age 11   Name Meghan M'Ara

Mouse

There once was a mouse
Who lived in a house
He climbed lots of trees
And ate lots of cheese

He went for a walk
and got eaten by a hawk
Now the Mouse who lived
in the house is gone

Eilidh Allen

Mice!!

Mice are hated,
coz they eat your grated cheese,
Mice are loved,
coz they eat your daughter's greer peas,
Mice are sneeky,
coz they get through doors + cracks,
I love mice coz they don't eat my snack!!!!

Luca. MacDonald
xx

The Mouse who played Music

Once, there was a mouse that lived a mouse in a house
He played lots of music and died, not really!
He played in an ochestra, he also
did magic and said tadot

the sausage mice © Rowan ®™ Simpson

Once upon a time there was a mouse called GILBERT.

He loved to eat sausage from FRANKFURT

He nibbled away for most of every DAY

Steering clear of the disgusting ~~cheese~~

He managed to live without FLEAS!

Rowan Simpson 14

In the cellar of the house,
There once lived a mouse,
Who ate of the scraps,
'Till he got stuck in the traps,
Now poor mouse lives on the street,
Getting drenched by the sleet,
Hoping he won't get crushed by someones feet,

The fate of a small mouse -
by Lucie Hall age 10

The mouse

Once there was a mouse
Who never lived in the same
house
He moved about everywhere
He even lived under the
stair
But then the cat came
And it started a game
To chase him right out
of the House.

Orla Stevens

The annoying mouse

There wus a mouse that wore a blouse I kicked it in the head, I went to bed it woke me up I broke his ribs and snapped his snout, he never bugged me again

by 🖋

aged 243,421,000

Just Hopeing

Hopeing they will not return
Their traps creaking and slaming
We live in fear of the future.

We just want food
A life to live
But to them we're better off dead

ORLA DICKSON   11

Mouse

Ye starving mouse oh what a shame
Oh dear yer dad that was quite lame
Yer sister's mister had nae bum
Yer brothers mother had no thumbs
I feel quite sad for your dad
Because he's gone stark raving mad
Would you like some tea? Oh yours is
And then youn must mouth need to pee
I end your sorrowful sad filled life
With the end of this knife
                    very sharp

Janine Steele

The mouse in the House

There once was a mouse
who lived in a house
It scurried over to the cheese

But one day there was a trap
And it went SNAP!!
Right on the little mouses
knees.

Rosie
MacLeod   Age: 12

The Cat (Mouse)

ooh!
cheese
~~red me those~~
but wait
~~The cat~~
if it sees me then
~~then~~ SNap
im trapped
in his terrable Jaws
one More ~~and in t~~
and im ~~too~~ scratched
by those so sharp,
Claws
Is it worth it
is it not
is it enugh
to risk getting caught
i think it is
~~im im~~ its not a trap
im doing well
SNap,

I am a Mouse

Oonagh Thin
Age 12

I am a mouse, not just an ordinary mouse,
I live in a palace, not a normal palace,
I live with the Queen, not any old queen,
I live with Elizabeth III!
I run through the halls,
I sneak in the kitchen,
I sleep in the bedroom,
I hide in the shoes,
I am a mouse, not an ordinary mouse!

CHEESE

Cheese Cheese Cheese!
Cheddar, Edam, Stilton and Brie
Those are the types that interest me!
My ears twitch
My whiskers twitch
YUM YUM YUM!
I love Cheese
Cheese loves me
OMG!

BJ Simpson 8 years old

Is there a mouse in your house

If there a mouse in your house
get out the trap and snap
we'll hope for the best
'ause there's a guest
Is there a mouse in your house?

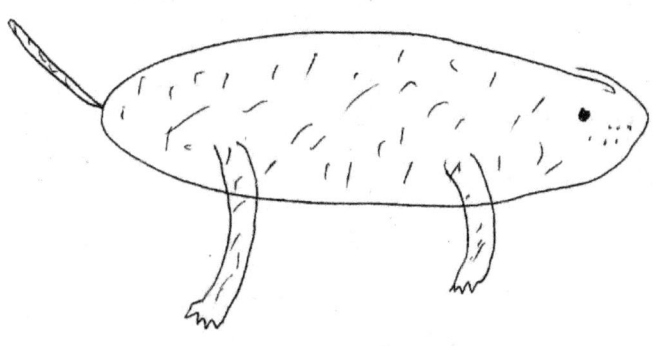

Felix Reynish   10 years old

Ben

There once was a mouse called Ben,
Who thought that he was a hen,
He went out to play,
With the chickens one day,
And has never been seen since then.

Catriona Hawksworth
Aged 12

Jack McPohhe age 17

There once was a mouse called BOB. It got eaten by a giant Hog. To be Continued...

MICE 1983

Oh give me strength,
I screamed as I tried to redeem
myself, catchin' mice is hard
and I'll save myself the bother,
I'll keep them as my pets and
let them nibble my toes.

Chrissy Bell age 7

There's a Mouse in my Chocolate mousse.

Mouse House

Far away there is a place
It's called a Mouse House
Unknown to all people
But known for all mice

Scampering and Squeeking
Foraging for food
Spreading chaos
Without being good

"Shoo mice, Shoo"
Is what the people say
That's why there is a Mouse House
So very far away

By Mia Scott.   Aged 11

Moose in the hoose

I was sitting in the hoose,
When along came a moose,
It scurried along the flair,
Eating things here and there,
Hello mouse, I said,
It said nothing, just ~~and~~ played dead
~~I should I needed the loo,~~
I was going to be late,
So I put some cheese on a plate,
~~The moose then ran over the floor,~~ and the moose
~~ate~~ ate and ate and ate

Charlie West, 12

Mice

Mice can be funny,
Much like a bunny
Although people wouldn't care if
there eaten by a bear,

They might be dumb, smart or smelly,
And if you let them they'd watch telly!
They are a wonder to the human kind
but you know they'd eat the cheese rind!

Lucy Girven (Age 12)

Run Run Little Mouse

Run Run Little mouse
Run Run Little mouse
Run Run Little mouse
Run Fast
Run Slow
Run Left
Run right
Run up
Run Down
Run Run Little mouse
before is to Late

by Ishbel   Age 11

That Mouse!

I mind my business
when out of the blue
a wee furry creature
comes out with no clue
that he is being watched
by me in my house
I jump on a chair
that creatures a mouse!
Ah well I guess it's just a mouse
I let it go in and out it's house.
NO WORRIES!

Seona Lee
12 Noble

Mouse

Mice eat rice.
Out they go "shooho" we all say.
Ugly though the fellow might taste like mellow

Jilly they are but not so pretty
Every one hates the

Eva.B
x x

Mouse Poem

~~There it goes~~ I see ~~the~~ Rachel, the mouse
~~Eating on my food~~
Scurring over the table
Not knowing I am watching
I move
It sees me
Back home it goes still eating.

Zoë Macintyre   Age - 16

Philosophy

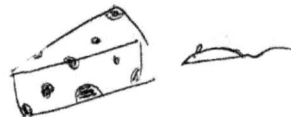

The question is: Do mice really like cheese?

aged: 13

Isabella Webster

The Mouse Trap

Maxim Bird

The ear-piercing squeak,
The loud click shut,
The cheese remains untouched,
The Predator becomes the victim
The trap has done its job.

The Mouse

Snap goes the trap,
waking up from the nap.
Run into the room
got to get that broom.
"That blasted mouse in my house!"

Kick it up from the floor.
It hits the door.
The broom goes woosh.
The cat goes Meaow
The mouse is now in
   Hell!

by Finn Croy   age 12

Wishful thinking

He crept slowly but surely right up to the edge,
There he now was, perched on the ledge.
Peering down he saw his glorious prize,
Left on a board inline with his eyes.
The creamy texture, and strong smell,
The object of his desire, oh it was swell!
But with a bang and a shout,
his dream went out.
After many a whining please,
the children ate his cheese.

Kirsty Glasgow, 17.

There's a moose aboot the hoose

Mice scurry

Out their wee hole

Upstairs in a hurry

Searching for the cat's bowl, and

Engulf in a flurry

Clare Sternitt AGE 14

The mouse
Runing up and
down.
Screaming to and
from
eating wahatever
founed.
hiding allover.

Luke Simpson 9

TRAP
Ewan Stewart 13

The room seemed to be empty,
No-one in sight at all,
It was all silent as i scurried out my hole,
I jump onto the table,
I jump towards my lunch,
munch, munch, munch munch, munch, munch, crunch,
Then with a twitch of my ears I hear someone coming,
I jump down from the table,
My heart pounding,
Searching for a hole,
For me to crawl,
My claws skitter though the hole,
Just in the nick of time,
 Snap goes the trap

MICE!

Mice are sneeky,
Mice are creepy,
Mice are hated,
Mice are fated,
Mice are dead,
Mice get in your bed,
mice are traped,
when they adopt

Kirsten. Simpson   12
xx

The Mouse

The mouse
ate a louse
and coughed up a cat
The cat was fat which killed a rat
The cats stomach rumbled
with discontent
cause he just got really spent
all he tasted
was the beer when he got wasted

Lachlan Riddell

The Creature

What is this creature that squeeks and squeals?
That ~~scurries at night~~
 Shivers and shakes
And makes its meals
From srumbs of stale cake?

What is this creature
That scratches the floors,
That scurries in ~~hols~~ cracks
That runs under doors
~~At~~ night in the black?

And wherever we see the twitch of a tail
An unexplained happening around the house
We remember the tale
Of the little old mouse

Phoebe O'Carroll-Moran 12

little stinkers

gnawing, stealing, ripping, chewing
When you have no food in the house
you must have a mouse or two or three.

The little stinkers sneak, poo & reak
That's all they do when their ridding your
house oh that wretched mouse.

I have a mouse in my bed, a mouse
that is dead, a mouse that shall rot,
and the made in to mouse soup stock

Angus Brownlie
10

THE BRAVE LITTLE MOUSE

A tiny grey ball of fur. It creeps out. It pitter patters across the floor. It's tiny feet quick and quiet. The twitching nose and swaying tail for it was even smaller than a snail. A peircing scream heard from up high, it scared the little creature and made it cry, but it stood it's ground and began to squeek, "please will you let me have something to eat?"

Naina Woodhouse. Age - 11 (2011)

The Sneeky Mouse in the house

There was a sneeky wee mouse in the house wich had a wee nose and tiny wee toes and loads and loads of louse. I got a trap and it ate my cap so I got tons of traps and stept on his toes.

Milly Hathway age 9

Society's Mouse

I run
I am being chased by a man with a gun
They want to kill me
I want to be free
Why can't they leave me be

I feel like a mouse
I have to get out of this house
I am weak and wee
They are close to catching me
Why can't they leave me be

They are closing in
My light is dim
They stamp on me with their elephant feet
The little mouse is getting beat

I under clapped
I got slapped
The mouse is trapped

Ben Morton   Age 15

The mouse in the house

Whats happening.....

No furry creatures scurrying along.

Oh no I see it. A creepy little mouse eating all our food. Quick get it before it goes everywhere round the house. Where is that horribly creature gone now. Uh Oh!

Laura Macleod
age 11

aw you wee sweet little mouse.

who knows what you dunken no one is here

No one knows what you ~~prefents~~ your favourit foods.

No one knows how you got here.
was it a struggle?
were you born here?
when evere you born anyway?
aw you wii sweet little mouse!

[W]ho knows?

by Sarah Ramsey

The moose

"AAAAA!! is that a moose I've seen?
Who's scampering around eating my beans?
Who's tail is long, and eyes are black,
Oh moose, do not come BACK!"

Imogen Reeves 11 years old

I know a Mouse

I know a mouse who has his own house
but he doesn't go in it because he has no kit
he goes in a bigger house and runs like a mouse
because he doesn't want to die or not even lie
he only wants some food so he can be in a better mood.

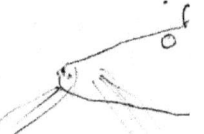

by sinead Thin age 10

Little Mouse

Tiny little mouse, don't be scared,
We're not going to hurt you, so you don't have to be prepared,
Your so petite, and absolutely sweet,
Though when your around, you run around our feet,
I would go to dogros and get a good cat, but you shouldn't be harmed,
So please respect that,

Ellen Francis aged 11

12/04/11. Death of a ginger mouse.

I once knew a ginger furred mouse. He lived in a hole in my house. He choked on some cheese and then started to weeze and died alone, outside in the breeze.

Rosaly Boyd.
14.
~~Boyd~~

Mini Mouse

Mini mouse get out of my house.

Off you run forever

Under the chair over the table

Soon as your back you will be in hat

Every where I go your always there, goodbye Mini mouse and away he flew.

Caitlin 12

12/04/11

The Mouse in the House

The mouse in our house makes such a racket,
It eats through every single packet.

We try and try to make it stop.
But nothing ever seemed to work.

                        Lucas Thomson
                        age: 9

Stupid Mice

They steal your food
Then chew your ice pucks
They cause no good
Then eat your best snacks

They have no good reason
And are always out of season
They are not nutritious
And don't taste nice

There isn't any point in those stupid Mice!

Euan "Shakespere" Brownlie

P.S I like cheese

Janie drew that

P.B Janie is a cartoonist

Mice

M ice
O n the table
U nder the stairs
S melly little things
E verywhere!

Name- Hansine Marshall
Age- 11

Mouse

I found it in ~~and~~ my shoe,
it smelt like it had been down
the loo,
it's tail was thin and springy,
as I raised my foot to damp
it down, scampering it went,
Running around live a clown.
I named it ~~B~~ Bob and he
became my best friend until
it got ran over by a JCB

THE WEE MOOSE

The tiny wee moose is in the hoose scittering and scattering away playing with it's tail and the cooks maid never will it get away.

As you see the moose astray you think where, how did it get here. As it scurrys away you think will it ever come back again.

By Freya Kuuskanen   Age: 10

The mouse and the Grouse had
a fight
the grouse thought the mouse stole
his light
the mouse gave it back, the
grouse gave him a pat
and they sat down for ~~bite~~
                              a bite

SQUIK

① There he is wrapped in a ball,
   Doesn't seem to move at all,
   Perhaps he's dead I'll just make sure,
   Pick this book up off the floor.

② Now he's flat and very round,
   Now he does not make a sound.
   No longer will he run round.
   He's embedded in the ground.

   Keir Hughes, 16

One day I saw a (HONEY) honey badger,
He was tiny, just a tadger,
To my greatest surprise,
He pointed to the skies
And took off like a winged Jammy Dodger.

KEIR HUGHES 16

11.   Mouse

Among the cracks in the wall there's
a wee beastie strange and small. Some
say he's a nuciance, some say a theif
but all that's he's looking for is a tasty
treat. We should not judge him for after
all, he's only small and really does not not
need much at all. Along the cracks in the
wall there was a wee beastie doing nothing wrong
at all.

Rhona Stevens   12 years old. !!

~~Soup and sandwiches tortho~~

<u>Soup & sandwiches</u>   Frances age...18

Soup & sandwiches! Lovingly made ~~prepared~~
for tutors, the whole morning they've played
on fiddle, piano, guitar and the drums,
now it's time for ~~tea~~ biscuits & buns.
We sit in the sun and eat up our food,
It all looks so lovely, ~~it~~ and it
tastes just as good.
Until now we are sitting, not feeling
so keen;
For we've just been told that a mouse
has been seen.
It inspected ~~the sandwich~~ salad, it sniffed
at the soup, it ~~nibb~~led the biscuits, ~~it~~
~~took~~ some samples it took. Maybe I'll bring my own lunch tomorrow...

108

Fat Mouse

The big Fat mouse lives in the big fat house, I saw him one day running out his big fat house I saw him run out onto the big fat plate of cookies I grabed him, I took him and put him in the oven I cooked him, I took him no longer was the big fat mouse fat he was as thin as a lace I took his head and made him dead and goodbye too my mouse.

Leonore age 9

The mouse who dide

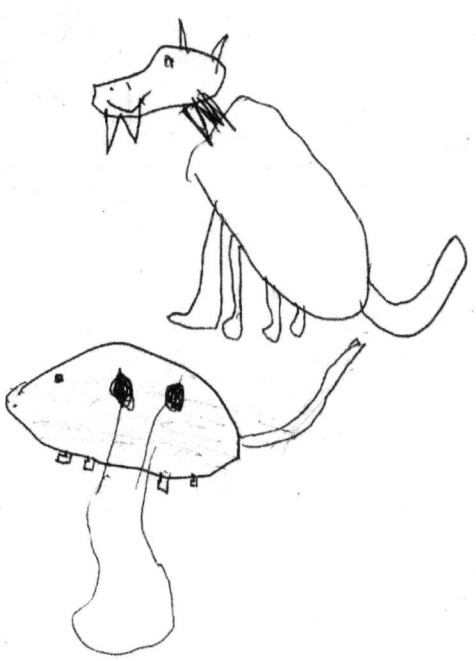

by Peter    Age 10

there ones was
a mouse who was
magick and was kild
by a muithnt cat
cacher

Hi poem

Mouse poem

The Scutteling mouse

The mouse scuttels though the pipes looking for food. ~~~~ every scrap of food lights up it's ~~~~ eyes in delite. but the mouse does not not know it ~~but~~ there's a cat at the edge of the table. the mouse

A Big fat Mouse

There was once a mouse
who wore a blouse unlike any
rodent in the world
He lost his blouse

Mouse

~~The naughty little mouse was once again stealing the stinky cheese.~~

~~A little mouse~~

A mouse small and naughty
was ~~crawling~~ walking along her kitchen floor.
She ~~was~~ small and thin,
but made lots of noise
~~She stole for the~~
E

Louise 13

The Poem Catcher And The Mouse

Though I guess the poem catcher is like a mouse,
Scavenging for poems instead of cheese,
His net like the wiskers ~~like the net~~ on a mouses cheek
And a hunger for a veriaty of food and poems.
They both wait for the food to be put on the table,
or put in the large collecting net or bag.
Though somtimes they get caught sometimes more painful than other times,
by raging police men or a deadly mouse trap.
But there is only one of the poem ~~catchers~~ and,
millions and millions of hungry mouses.
But what is there more food or poems.

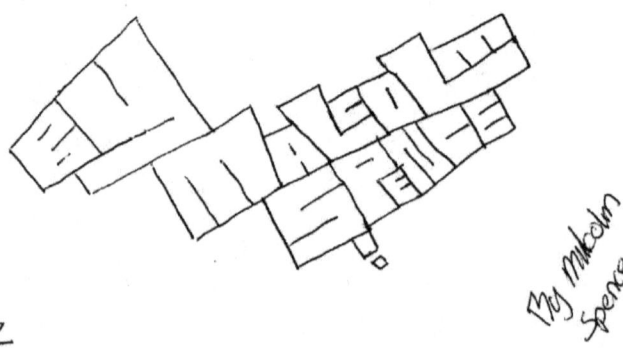

By Malcolm Spence

SKATZ

Mouse!

Mouse, mouse, mouse, mouse,
I am a mouse!
mice and mouse, mouse and mice.
Mouse, Mouse, mouse, mouse <u>MICE!</u>

by Lois age 12

MICE

Mice don't like bees
But they do like cheese
Mice are'nt so nice unless they're in Dyce
Thats because they sell alot of rice.
They like rice cause its made of ice
And they like ice cause its made of mice
        THE END

        James Girven age 9

Society's Mouse

I run
I am being chased by a man with a gun
They want to kill me
I want to be free
Why can't they leave me be

I feel like a mouse
I have to get out of this house
I am weak and wee
They are close to catching me
Why can't they leave me be

They are closing in
My light is dim
They stamp on me with their elephant feet
The little mouse is getting beat

Thunder clapped
I got slapped
The mouse is trapped

Ellen Morton   Age 15

Mice eat rice, but for them it doesn't taste nice. It's a big price for the lice, who only eat dice with ice

Write your poem here...

www.ingramcontent.com/pod-product-compliance
Lightning Source LLC
Chambersburg PA
CBHW052027290426
44112CB00014B/2405